Regulation:
Its Impact on Decision Making

By Ronald Berenbeim
Research Associate

A Research Report from The Conference Board

Contents

Tables

Author's Acknowledgments

The author wishes to thank the Conference Board Staff colleagues who assisted at various stages of the project. Earl Bailey, Patrick Davey, Leonard Lund, Mitchell Meyer, Ruth Shaeffer and Francis J. Walsh were helpful with the technical aspects of the legislative areas examined. The development of an interview format was considerably aided by Allen Janger.

About This Report

THE IMPACT of government regulation on the management process, as opposed to its business costs, has been largely overlooked. This study explores changes that have occurred in the decision-making process as a consequence of regulation. Specifically, it attempts to discern changes in the locus of decision-making authority, and changes in the relative roles of those involved in the network of actions affected by regulation.

Highlights

Regulation has had the overall effect of pushing companies toward a greater degree of centralization in areas subject to compliance or review. The effect is most pronounced in certain equal employment and environmental issues, but far less so in the areas of employee safety, cost accounting standards, advertising and warranties.

In most companies, this shift toward centralization has been accomplished by:

(1) Enunciating new policies, procedures and/or other administrative constraints, or by further detailing existing policies. Although most companies surveyed had already established policies in the covered areas, the onset of regulation caused at least one-third of them to add constraints. In the case of EEOC, four out of five companies did so, while two out of three added them in the environmental area.

(2) Involving more people in the decision-making network. Prior consultation, review and/or approval are far more the order of the day in the areas affected by regulation. Again, the changes are most evident in EEOC and environmental areas, less so in cost accounting standards, and near the 50 percent mark with respect to OSHA, ERISA, and FTC regulation on warranties.

(3) Moving authority to take action and to make decisions up the corporate ladder. With the exception of decisions on EEOC, most companies chose not to take this path. Even so, the number that did is substantial.

Characteristically, companies use at least two of these devices; for example, adding constraints plus more consultation. Only the smaller companies—those with less than $250 million in sales—rely more heavily on moving authority to a higher level.

To assure regulatory compliance, a majority of the companies surveyed employ an individual at the corporate level to spend full or part time on compliance activity within specific areas of regulation. Few, however, have set up a committee or designated an official to coordinate or oversee all compliance activities.

The survey reveals explosive growth in company legal departments. One of five of the companies established a legal department during the past ten years; most of the others increased its size. Indeed, the median size more than doubled—from three to seven—during the ten-year period. The heaviest involvement of legal staff is in the area of consumer regulations.

With the major exceptions of EEOC and the enviromental regulation, the perceived impact of regulation in the areas studied is judged "moderate"; but these perceptions vary by the size of company and industry. OSHA is judged more "severe" among smaller than larger companies, but had minimal effects on financial firms; environmental regulations were singled out by utilities and the largest companies.

On more specific effects, most feel that regulation has slowed the decision-making process. Despite more centralization, most see no adverse impact on management development. A major adverse effect cited, however, is in foreign competition: three out of five—preponderantly the manufacturing companies—profess impaired ability to compete against foreign firms.

Regulatory Areas Studied

In order to assess the impact of regulation with some precision, nine hypothetical decisions involving regulatory exposure in key areas—EEOC, OSHA, ERISA, environmental, consumer, and cost accounting standards—were selected. A mailed questionnaire asked the participants to analyze, for each hypothetical decision, how that decision was made prior and subsequent to regulatory intervention. The focus of examination was the extent of involvement of various corporate departments and personnel, and the use of policy constraints. In addition to analyzing hypothetical situations, respondents answered specific questions about various aspects of the company's operations relevant to the regulatory process, such as the general counsel's office, the use of outside organizations—law firms, industry associations—and so forth for help in dealing with compliance problems.

From the outset, it was recognized that many companies would not find certain hypothetical questions relevant to their own situations. Indeed, that proved to be the case; banks, for example, frequently indicated that safety legislation was not a major problem. Nonetheless, a sizable response was obtained for all the hypothetical questions, and many companies found that each question raised issues that continue to be pertinent to their particular enterprise.

Source of the Data

Four hundred and one companies completed and returned the questionnaire. Interviews were conducted with executives (including CEO's) in a representative sample of companies around the country. At some companies more than one person was interviewed. Respondents included a cross section of individuals who might be concerned with aspects of the regulatory process—for example, CEOs, Vice President-Public Affairs, General Counsel, Vice President-Personnel, Director-Government Accounting Policy, and Director-Organizational Planning.

Nearly three-quarters of the participants were manufacturing companies, financial institutions and utilities accounted for a fifth of the companies. Retail establishments, construction and mining firms also responded.

The firms surveyed are predominantly middle-sized to large companies, with a median employee population of 5,500 and median sales of $556 million. The range in size, however, is considerable: from a low of 120 employees and $15 million in sales, to a high of 405,000 employees and over $46 billion in sales.

Foreword

THE IMPACT OF REGULATION on business has been a highly discussed topic in recent years. While the subject has received considerable attention, most of that analysis has focused on the cost to business of complying with specific regulations.

Beyond the cost impact, the regulatory environment—created in large measure by federal legislation which was enacted and implemented in the previous decade—has also had a lasting effect on the business process.

These changes in the way business is actually conducted form the subject matter of this report. More specifically, how has the manager's job changed now that regulation is exposing his or her decisions to ever-increasing scrutiny? What has happened to the manager's discretion, which in the past had been exercised in the name of greater decentralization?

Participants in this study are of the view that regulation has had a significant impact on the management process. Within this general outlook a variety of emphases can be found; for some the critical impact has been actual structural changes—a decision is now made at a higher level, or additional persons or policies must be consulted before a decision is made. Others feel that new attitudes brought on by the regulatory environment have been more important than any shifts in authority. This diversity of responses shows that there are many different ways in which regulatory pressure has altered management's role.

The Conference Board wishes to thank those executives who gave freely of their time to describe candidly the difficulties and challenges faced by business institutions in responding to the regulatory explosion of the last decade.

This study is a product of the Management Research Division, Harold Stieglitz, Vice President, and is part of the Board's Business-Government Research Program, E. Patrick McGuire, Executive Director.

KENNETH A. RANDALL
President

Chapter 1
The New Era of Regulation: An Overview

REGULATION DOES NOT ALWAYS mean the same thing to different observers, although it has become the subject of heated discussion. At the heart of what most people mean when they talk about regulation are the operations of federal regulatory agencies, such as the Environmental Protection Administration, and others. These federal agencies are established by statute and given broad regulatory powers to achieve the underlying objectives of the statute; for example, clean air, occupational safety, and equal employment opportunity, among others.

While this is the dominant regulatory model, it is by no means the only one. Executive Orders from state governors and the President often have regulatory consequences. Trade policy can also create an environment that fits a regulatory model in terms of business behavior. Probably the overwhelming volume of regulation with which business must contend is still at the state and local level— zoning, licensing, safety requirements—issues in which local interests and competence remain paramount.

Despite what continues to be the predominantly local nature of most regulation, it is federal regulation that has aroused the most intense emotions. It is also the variety of regulation that has undergone the most radical change in character during the past decade. Indeed, a brief history of federal regulation would show that the 1970's were a decade apart in the evolution of the federal regulatory process, the beginning of a fourth era in a still-evolving federal approach to the regulation of commerce.

Historical Background

We can best understand major phases in regulatory evolution by discerning the particular relationships the federal apparatus sought to examine and direct at various times in our history.

1

During the first century (up to 1887), the federal establishment focused its regulatory powers on the states. Federal regulation sought to assist business by promoting the free flow of commerce and preventing undue discrimination by one state against goods produced by the others.

With the establishment of the Interstate Commerce Commission in 1887 (the first independent regulatory commisson), the Federal Government began to concentrate on the relationship between competing businesses, rather than competing states. The Interstate Commerce Commission was established primarily to prevent discrimination in rate making by carriers against those businesses competing for their services. For nearly half a century, until the coming of the New Deal in 1933, the underlying objective of federal regulation was to ensure fair rules of competition among rival businesses.

The legislation emanating fron Franklin Roosevelt's New Deal focused regulatory powers on the relationship between business and the client or consumer. Beginning with the Securities Act of 1933, the honesty and the fairness of the transaction between a business and its customers became the subject of regulatory scrutiny. An underlying assumption of much of this legislation was the view that the bargaining relationship between a single consumer and a large business was inherently unequal, and that the classical contractual rules required a certain amount of legislative redress in this context.

The most recent phase in the evolution of federal regulation began with the passage of the Civil Rights Act of 1964. With that legislation, and its strict enforcement and implementation during the 1970's, federal regulation turned to an examination of the business process, and began to require evidence that this process was consistent with broadly defined social and moral objectives, such as equal employment opportunity and clean air and water.

Impact of the Regulatory Explosion

If there is some vagueness as to what is meant by "regulation," there is an equal amount of confusion when business leaders talk about its "effects." The effects of regulation on American business, particularly the new regulations of the 1970's, are widely believed to be severe. "Regulation" per se has become a hot issue and, in the view of many, responsible for much—if not all—of what has gone wrong with American industry.

For a significant minority of executives the words "cost" and "effect" are interchangeable. One company president states bluntly: "If you were in control before, the thing changing is cost." Any number of business leaders would agree with the assessment that the primary effect of regulation on both business and the larger American community has been "greater costs." Nonetheless, many of those interviewed believe the impact goes beyond "cost." Moreover, in the view of a substantial number, at least some of the costs of regulation are worth paying. One of these executives summarized this outlook in a story worth quoting in detail: "A couple of nights ago I took my son to a baseball game and a foul ball hit into the stands and injured a woman spectator. That whole episode got me to thinking about the risks society will accept, as against the risks it will not accept. Everyone who goes to a baseball game knows that they might be hit by a baseball. Yet they do not expect the government to move in and minimize or eliminate this risk.

"Still, it is clear there are some hazards the people want minimized or eliminated by intervention of this sort. Opinion surveys show great public commitment to clean air and water—even in hard times. No one really knows the long-run costs, but thus far there has been an amazing willingness to pay them. Even if the public knew the full cost, they still might be willing to pay them. Our people [his company's employees] are part of society, too. To a significant extent, they share these values and have accepted them to a greater degree than they did as recently as five years ago. No person in this company wants another Love Canal. What it comes down to is how you define 'standard of living.' For many of us, it's not just costs of production and productivity, it is clean air and water as well."

Still, this executive observes, not everyone in his company agrees with this view and he states: "For the younger people societal objectives like clean air and water have been internalized. Many of them have engineering backgrounds and look at regulatory requirements as technical problems to be solved. They do not question whether a rule should be followed. Older people ask why something should be done. They are proud of their profession. They think they did a good job. Now people are telling them they did things wrong. They do not buy that. Still, there is not much doubt that young and old alike appreciate changes like clean air."

The response of individual companies—as opposed to business in general—to governmental regulation has not followed any single or predictable pattern. With some companies it has required complex and far-reaching change; with others it has done little but "increase costs." While the adjustments mandated by the regulatory explosion of the last decade have been the subject of much criticism from business, they also have their quiet defenders within corporations. Thus, when the focus is on *particular* regulations and what they *actually require the company to do,* the real impact that regulation has had on companies becomes more evident.

Regulatory Areas Examined

In order to determine the impact that selected regulatory changes of the 1970's have had on management, The Conference Board focused on nine areas of regulatory activity. Respondents were given hypothetical situations and asked how those would be handled and if their approach had changed, now that such decisions were subject to regulatory review. What follows is a brief description of the various regulatory areas chosen for examination.

Equal Employment Opportunity Commission

The 1964 Civil Rights Act established the Equal Employment Opportunity Commission (EEOC) to seek voluntary conciliation among the parties with respect to complaints of discrimination based on race, color, religion, sex or national origin. In addition, the Commission issued guidelines as to compliance standards under the law. In 1972, Title VII of the Equal Employment Act of 1964 was amended, increasing the powers of the Commission to file civil suits against parties violating the Act's provisions.

The Commission announced that it would treat all complaints as "class actions." As a consequence, a judgment in favor of one employee could lead to remedies for others similarly situated. As has proven to be the case in a number of other areas examined by this study, Federal legislation provided the impetus for considerable state and local regulation in those regions of the country where discrimination in employment had not previously been subject to regulation. (The conflict between these state-local regulatory demands and federal standards has been a recurring problem.)

Occupational Safety and Health Act

Occupational safety and health are the subjects of this legislation which was passed in 1970. The bill requires compliance with both specific safety procedures that have been developed for the applicable industry, and general health and environmental standards for the workplace. Employers are subject to periodic inspections, and must provide reports to appropriate governmental departments on an annual basis.

Employee Retirement Income Security Act

The Employee Retirement Income Security Act of 1974 (ERISA), establishes safeguards for the security of pension funds. (According to those questioned, if ERISA's demands ended there, far fewer complaints would be directed against it.) ERISA's requirements, however, are twofold: they mandate what a company *must do* to establish the security of its pension program (not a matter of great controversy) and, secondly, what a company *must say* it is doing in reports to employees and the government. It is the latter reporting demand which is said to have had the greatest impact on the organization studied.

Environmental Protection Legislation

Environmental regulation (unlike most of the other areas) is not the product of a single piece of legislation, but rather the result of several major regulations enforced by the Environmental Protection Agency. This study focuses primarily on air and water pollution control requirements.

4

Regulatory compliance with environmental standards is the major area in which conflict between state and local standards creates significant problems.

Consumer Product Safety Act

The legislation enacted in 1972 has the dual purpose of promoting the gathering and distributing of data on causes and preventions of consumer product defects, and protecting the public through the establishment of safety standards for various consumer products. To achieve these legislative objectives, the government has established requirements with respect to the labeling, testing and statements of conformity to applicable product standards. In addition, the five-member Consumer Product Safety Commission has the power to seek a court declaration that a product is an "imminent hazard," or to find as a result of its own investigation that a product is a "substantial hazard." In the first instance, the remedy may be seizure and condemnation; in the latter, it is modification, replacement, repair or refund.

Magnuson-Moss Federal Trade Commission Improvement Act

The first portion of this 1972 statute is concerned with minimum standards for product warranties. The Act requires that warranties be designated as either "full" or "limited" and that the disclaimers of implied warranties be limited. It also establishes procedures for the FTC's examination of warranties and for the settling of warranty disputes.

Truth in Lending Act and Various Amendments

The Truth in Lending Act of 1969, as amended in 1974, requires that banks and credit institutions make full and accurate disclosures of credit terms. It guarantees the consumer redress in the event that these standards are not met.

Truth in Advertising

Unlike most of the other major regulatory areas examined, the requirements for compliance with the objectives of "truth in advertising" regulations do not emanate from a specific statute, but rather from the Federal Trade Commission's rule-making authority. The most important developments in this area began in 1971 with the establishment of a rule requiring advertisers to submit to the FTC, on demand, materials substantiating a "product's safety, performance, efficacy, quality, or comparative price."

The Cost Accounting Standards Board

The Cost Accounting Standards Board is an agency of Congress created in 1970 to establish rules for computing the cost elements of defense contracts in excess of $100,000. The General Services Administration subsequently amended federal procurement regulations to apply cost accounting standards to most nondefense contracts in excess of $100,000. The 1970 law requires contractors to comply with federal cost accounting standards in pricing contract proposals and in the reporting of their performance under such contracts.

Chapter 2
Regulation: Impact on the Management Process

IN A SENSE, regulations have at least two substantially different, albeit overlapping, impacts on a company:

(1) Impact on the company's operations, that is, its markets, its products, and its ability to compete.

(2) Impact on the management process, that is, its organization, its decision-making process, and the "culture" within which those decisions are made.

Much of the impact of regulation on the latter—the management process—is focused on cost considerations. These added costs usually result from the additional people, paper and time required to meet regulatory requirements.

For example, several years ago, Armco Steel, in its annual report, noted that the cost of paperwork in connection with a $10 license payment for heavy trucks at one of their plants was $1,240. Armco's request to pay a $25 fee in lieu of supplying this information was turned down.

However, a substantial dimension not included in quantifiable "costs" is the resultant change in what one executive calls the internal "barriers, rituals and procedures" that action-oriented executives experience in doing their work. How does regulation and regulatory scrutiny change the management process? In the sometimes ambiguous language of management and organization, the general corporate response is quite straightforward: "The effect of increased regulation has been to decentralize the implementation of decisions and to centralize the review, approval and ratification of those decisions."

Response to this question had an impressive consistency: the agreement rate of 75 percent held for companies both large and small, and for high- and low-growth organizations. Only among 21 very small companies (under

7

$100 million in sales) was there a significantly lower level of agreement with this statement.

A major purpose of this study is to reduce the ambiguous terms centralization-decentralization to specifics. Do the same people still have the same degree of responsibility for initiating and making decisions? Are additional reviews and approvals called for before implementing decisions? Are more functionaries, specialists, et al required? If so, where? Put even more simply, who are the new actors and actresses and what parts do they play? In the language of Hollywood, has a low budget, intimate drama become a blockbuster with a cast of thousands? Are the new players stars, supporting cast, or do they merely have walk-on parts?

Documenting and analyzing these kinds of changes is difficult because of the nuances of corporate process and etiquette. Position guides and linear responsibility charts may suggest that decision making is segregated into orderly, discreet stages whereby one person has authority for making a decision, another for its review and approval, and a third for its implementation. In practice, however, the rules of the game may be substantially different.

Presumed lines of authority are invariably muted. The boss may still be the boss, but the power to countermand initiatives is best held in reserve for extraordinary circumstances. Better still is creating a situation where it does not have to be exercised at all. Modern management tries, wherever possible, to facilitate rather than command. For this reason there appears to be a heavy reliance on policy restraints to secure compliance with regulatory mandates. This is a practice consistent with the trend toward a more democratic and participative management process, "a government of laws and not of men." It is far easier to obtain obedience to impersonal policy demands than to the edict of single individuals.

Still, to paraphrase President Truman's observation, the buck has to stop somewhere. Though they do not like to do it, management will concede, when pressed, that certain persons do have authority to initiate or decide upon an action; others may have to be consulted before action is taken, and, finally, yet another individual may have to ratify or approve the decision.

Indeed, in discussions with executives, it becomes clear that they can discern several ways in which the authority delegated to them and their roles in the decision-making process tend to be altered and/or circumscribed:

(1) Most obvious, of course, is the transfer of authority to make few, some or all decisions to a higher level in the organization. This is centralization in the classic sense of the term. It happens for a variety of reasons, only one of which may be the increased risk involved in regulatory-affected decisions.

(2) Less obvious, but far more prevalent in the experience of the managers surveyed, is the insertion of what was previously described as

"barriers and rituals." The nominal authority of any position may be great, but the actual authority varies to the extent that the individual must consult with or seek approval or ratification from others. Similarly, the necessity of reporting on activities, where no previous reports were required, becomes an incursion on some managers' freedom or authority to act.

(3) Least obvious, possibly because it is almost taken for granted, are policies and procedures that are a major means of management control.

The Push to Centralization

Regardless of whether the entity in question is a nation or a business, the characteristic response to external pressure is centralization of authority. External pressure often escalates risk, and decisions and actions having high-risk consequences tend to move up the ladder of decision making. Most of the executives surveyed say that the current regulatory environment poses the kinds of external challenges that have a centralizing effect.

The regulatory explosion of the 1970's is believed to have created a system of external limitations that go beyond the conventional considerations of sound business policy. The possibility of third-party review of such day-to-day business practices as hiring, firing, equipment purchases, pension funding, and product recall can limit an executive's freedom of action. Potential corporate liability generates concern among top management that decisions subject to regulatory exposure receive adequate review within the company. What is more, top management control is exercised through policies that enunciate the company's commitments as well as obligations under regulatory legislation.

Control, in a management context, is the power to determine these factors that have a bearing on a managerial decision. The need to consult new policies and procedures, or to ask staff personnel for interpretations of policy or governmental regulations, reduces a manager's authority. The authority to draft corporate standards, policies and procedures can determine in an impersonal way the real parameters of all future actions in a given area. Moreover, in ways not yet totally understood, the power to interpret the limitations imposed by particular regulations or policies may now be the real sum and substance of management power. As a consequence, the appearance of authority may remain, while its substance, in slow imperceptible and, perhaps, even unintentional ways, is dispersed to other parts of the organization.

These three changes can operate separately or can be combined to create an aura of increased centralization. And it is usually senior management, in the person of the CEO, who determines the degree of centralization. For example:

(1) At a minimum, the message that comes through is: "It is desirable to comply with regulations in this area"; or a more pragmatic: "We will

operate in a manner that keeps us out of trouble with the regulatory bodies.''

(2) A more restrictive stance would go beyond a generalized "policy" to include more specific guidelines or procedures. In this approach, top management's position may be: "It is desirable to comply with regulation, and this is how we believe we ought to do it."

(3) Still more restrictive is the use of monitoring after the fact. It adds up to: "It is desirable to comply, this is how it ought to be done, and the staff will be checking to see how effectively the policy of compliance is implemented."

(4) And most restrictive of all is a system that states: "Compliance is a corporate objective. This is how we will do it. Consult with and check all major decisions with appropriate functional heads to make sure that they are consistent with this policy, and staff will be checking to see how effectively this policy is implemented."

Most of those interviewed characterized their companies as being in the third category—"functional control" was a term used—and they saw few differences in the kind of delegation used to achieve regulatory compliance among the various areas under examination. But even among those companies using a less restrictive form of delegation, there is general agreement that top management now requires more in the way of reporting and auditing than it did before various areas were subject to regulation. Most of those interviewed expect even more in the way of top management controls as the regulatory process becomes more of a fact of life in the company. "As the years go by, we are going to move right down that list," said one executive.

Still, not every chief executive is in that much of a hurry to roll up his or her sleeves and get on with compliance. One executive of a company run in a highly personal style comments: "The boss takes a different view. With the exception of EEOC, where the company has made important gains which he recognizes, he thinks that regulation is baloney, and he believes in resistance, wherever it is legal. He thinks that business is doing a good job of meeting the needs of employees, and that the best thing for people is a good, safe job. Still, if a bill becomes law, we follow it, so I guess you could say we are in the first category of companies."

Although most executives believe that their firms' approach to delegation of authority is reasonably consistent, regardless of the area of delegation, perceptions sometimes vary when more than one person from the same company is interviewed. One manager, who has responsibility for environmental compliance at a major oil company, observes: "We are moving from an enabling system of controls [category 1] to the guideline approach [category 2], and I think we are going to have even more auditing of compliance in the future. I have discussed that very point with the chief executive of the company.'

Another individual, whose responsibilities are in the area of energy-regulation compliance, states that at his company tight control is generally the case, particularly with respect to Department of Energy regulations. "This has been true since 1971 when I became involved in this area," he says. "There was greater decentralization before. Local pricing managers made the decisions for their markets, there were no allocation issues at that time."

In one instance, a company spokesman believes that the issue of delegation has not been greatly affected by increased governmental regulation. This executive, the assistant to the president of one of the country's fastest growing companies, says: "We want to comply, but the responsibility for compliance has to be delegated. People come back and touch base. The president is the kind of guy that wants to know everything that is going on. He does not have to check. There is more delegation now because of our size, not because of regulation. Our growth has been tremendous."

Still, most of those questioned agree that regulation—not growth—is the real reason for greater restraint or control. At least one executive had first-hand experience with the reasons for a centralization of authority in a company. He says: "I would characterize our system as having tight controls in all areas. This has been true for 12 years, ever since we were burned, and burned badly, in our handling of a consumer issue. Before that we used the enabling approach [category 1], but that bad experience really had an effect on us. That one episode resulted in the conversion of an old-line company into a tightly run organization with modern management controls. These controls were needed in other aspects of our operations as well, and now we have them."

In some companies, the change to accommodate regulation occurs formally. The company, in effect, issues directives of a "now hear this" quality. In others, the change occurs informally: There is a general recognition that regulation requires different modes of communication and decision making; common sense dictates changes; and individuals accommodate to new external realities.

The Pragmatic Consequences

The organizational structure that develops for making decisions in this "negotiated environment" is, and will continue to be, the product of experience and pragmatic adaptation to constantly changing necessities (see Table 1).

As of now, companies participating in the survey indicate that, relative to the nine areas of regulation studied, regulatory reality has dictated varying degrees of change, depending upon the area regulated. A majority of the changes have been in terms of adding prior consultation and advice and/or policy or procedural constraints. Thus, with respect to the decisions examined by the survey, the dominant response (with the exception of actions

Table 1: Changes in Decision-making Authority within the Company

Regulatory Area	Decision at a Higher Level		Number of Departments Involved Has Increased		Company Has More Administrative Constraints	
	Number of Companies	Percent of Companies	Number of Companies	Percent of Companies	Number of Companies	Percent of Companies
EEOC	226	59%	298	78%	312	82%
OSHA	82	23	173	49	177	50
ERISA	105	28	165	45	189	52
Environmental	144	44	236	73	214	67
Consumer Safety	113	44	150	59	139	56
FTC-Warranties	84	33	119	48	111	45
Truth in Lending	73	25	117	40	120	42
Advertising	93	27	135	39	143	42
Cost Accounting	62	24	91	36	87	35

involving potential EEOC exposure) is that the level of position or unit that now has decision-making authority is essentially the same as it was prior to the passage of legislation. However, in a significant minority of cases for each of the hypothetical decisions posed, the level of position or unit that now has ultimate authority is higher. The exception to this general rule involves actions dealing with equal opportunity questions. In this area, the dominant response is to delegate the responsibilty to a higher level.

Changing Levels of Authority

As noted, shifting responsibility to someone higher in the chain of command is not the form of organizational centralization most frequently adopted (except for EEOC). Environmental and consumer product-safety decisions are made by a higher-level official nearly half the time; in other areas approximately one-third to one-fourth of the businesses have shifted regulatory-affected decisions upward. Despite a clear preference for giving operational-level executives wide latitude in decision making, when regulatory review becomes a possibility, many companies prefer to reserve responsibility for certain actions to persons occupying a higher rung on the corporate ladder.

Two of the more common approaches in this upward shift are the involvement of additional persons or units for consultation and review, and establishment of new policies and procedures to assure regulatory compliance. These methods are used by the companies studied with nearly the same degree of frequency (see Table 1). At least one-third of those surveyed report that they had made one of the latter types of adjustment.

Reflecting on most firms' preferences for leaving the responsibility for initiating action where it had been in the past, but subjecting that action to a higher level of review, or additional policy constraints, an executive of one of the country's largest corporations states: "Our style of business is that it is management's responsibility to do what is necessary. Each individual must get things done—regulation included. Although we have EEOC coordinators, the lowest ranking manager or first-line supervisor has the primary responsibility for a decision. To give you an example: As a manager I have my own responsibilities for EEOC. If I have a vacancy, I try to fill it with a minority applicant if I can. Ordinarily, that is my responsibility. But let us say the person I can fill the vacancy with is not promotable. The company has a policy of not hiring such individuals. In that case I would consult with the EEOC coordinator and my boss to resolve the variance between two conflicting company policies. On the one hand we do not hire people who are not promotable; on the other, we have important affirmative action goals which are also company policy."

Policies: More Rather Than New

Policies and procedures, as a means of assuring that decisions relative to regulation are in compliance with the statutes, warrant particular mention. They are by no means new; but in most companies, as indicated in Table 1, regulation has required a more detailed or exacting spelling out of these administrative constraints. Because the goal of a particular piece of regulatory legislation is often one for which there is a broad consensus, even if the means of achieving it cannot be agreed upon, it is not surprising that many companies had already established programs and/or policies for dealing with certain problem areas.

Many of those interviewed agreed with the executive who said: "Regulation has not caused us to do anything additional to protect the public—because we were already doing what regulation requires us to do. Regulation just requires more dotting of i's and crossing of t's." Survey data lend support to this assertion (see Table 2). In every major regulatory area examined by the study, a majority of companies had instituted some sort of policy or administrative constraint—such as rules on the dismissal of an employee, or safety requirements for the use of certain machinery, prior to the demands imposed by regulation.

The differences among the various areas with respect to pre-regulatory involvement is instructive. A smaller percentage of companies had policy constraints in equal employment, safety, and air and water pollution control than in other areas. That is probably why equal employment opportunity and environmental protection were the areas of regulation mentioned most frequently by those interviewed as those in which regulation has compelled changes to deal with these issues. Yet even in the area of equal employment, nearly two-thirds of the companies surveyed had some sort of policy constraint prior to regulation.

Variations by Area of Regulation

As already indicated, the changes vary with the specific areas of regulation. The following sections examine each of these nine areas separately.

Equal Employment Opportunity Commission

Equal employment opportunity regulation has had the most pervasive administrative impact of any of the regulations examined by the study. Nearly half of the 400-plus companies indicate that they had made all three of the previously discussed changes, and almost one-fifth had made two of the changes for any decision to terminate the employment of minority or female personnel.

Thus, nearly three-quarters of the companies surveyed have made at least two of the three possible changes in the decision-making process. The extent and nature of these changes varies with company size. The smaller the company, the more likely it is to rely on shifting the decision level upward. The larger companies often rely upon new guidelines and/or greater staff

Table 2: Extent of Company Constraints Prior to Regulation

Regulatory Area	Had Prior Constraints	No Prior Constraints	Percent with Prior Constraints
EEOC	225	153	60%
OSHA	230	120	66
ERISA	271	91	75
Environmental Protection	205	113	64
Consumer Protection	185	66	74
Consumer Warranties	181	63	74
Truth in Lending	203	80	72
Truth in Advertising	243	95	72
Cost Accounting Standards	166	86	66

specialist involvement and consultation. The change least likely to be made in larger firms was to transfer authority for decisions to a higher level.

Occupational Safety and Health Administration

Compared with certain other areas, OSHA's administrative impact on the companies surveyed is more modest. Of the 356 organizations that stated that an equipment purchase decision was relevant to their company's operations, one-third reported that there has been no change in the process since OSHA.[1] Slightly more than one-sixth of the companies, however, have raised the level of authority for making the decision, involve additional persons in review and approval of contemplated action, and have developed policies concerning these issues. Another one-fifth of the companies surveyed have made the last two of these three changes. Manufacturing companies are, of course, the industrial group primarily affected, and the larger the company, the more likely it is that some, or all, of these changes will have been made.

Employee Retirement Income Security Act

ERISA, like OSHA, has had a comparatively mild administrative impact. One-third of the 366 companies responding reported no change in the procedure for selecting a pension fund manager. One-sixth of the respondents, however, made all three changes, while another one-sixth involved have made two changes—additional personnel and new policy regulations. ERISA's effects vary according to company size and type. Financial companies are more likely to make serious adjustments than are manufacturers;

---

[1] One of the hypothetical decisions subject to regulatory review.

utilities, on the other hand, are less likely to make major changes. ERISA has had the most serious administrative impact on middle-sized companies.

Environmental Protection

Next to equal opportunity, environmental regulation has had the most severe effect on the decision-making process. Close to two-fifths of the 325 companies that reported on their decisions on environmental issues said they had made all three of the major administrative changes. More than one-fourth had made two of them (involvement of additional personnel, new policies and/or procedures). Less than one-fifth reported no change in prior practices in the hypothetical decision which asked about company procedure for developing a waste-disposal plan. Virtually all of the respondents in this area were either manufacturers or utilities.

Although the administrative impact of environmental legislation on manufacturers was considerable (60 percent added policy constraints, and now involve additional persons in the development of waste-disposal plans, and two-thirds of those have also raised the level of final responsibility in this area), changes were even more pervasive among utilities—three-quarters had made the first two changes, and over half had also pushed the responsibility for a decision to a higher level. As to size, larger companies are more likely to have made changes than are smaller ones.

Finally, companies that feel that the effect of environmental regulation has been only "moderate" are nearly as likely to have made serious administrative changes as those who consider it to be "severe." In other areas, perception of severity and degree of administrative change were more directly correlated.

Consumer Protection

Questions concerning various types of consumer regulation, consumer product safety, FTC improvement act (1975) (establishing criteria for warranties), truth in advertising, and truth in lending elicited fewer responses, for the most part, than other areas. The exception was the truth-in- advertising question which generated 344 responses. With the exception of consumer product safety, consumer regulation generated significantly fewer administrative changes than EEOC or environmental legislation. Still, at least one-fifth of the respondents made all three organizational changes in response to the FTC improvement act, truth in advertising, or truth in lending, and 10 percent or more in each case now involve more personnel and have policy directives for decisions affected by these regulations. The variation from this pattern of relatively weak effect involves 253 companies on which consumer product-safety regulations have an impact. Here the administrative changes have been nearly as widespread as with equal employment and environmental regulations. Over one-third of the respondents made all three administrative changes, and another 14 percent established new policy regulations and involved additional personnel in product recall decisions.

Only scattered answers were received from nonmanufacturing companies in the consumer product-safety and warranty areas. The truth-in-lending and truth-in-advertising questions, however, revealed that financial institutions are more likely to make serious administrative changes than are manufacturers. In general, company size is not a serious predictor of administrative change.

Cost Accounting Standards Board

Cost accounting standards, like consumer regulation, affected a smaller percentage of respondents than more pervasive regulations like EEOC. Most of the 254 companies that did respond were manufacturers, so that no distinctions can be made among industry groups. Over one-sixth of the respondents made all three of the structural changes in their decision-making process, and another 9 percent now involve addiitional personnel and have policy regulations in decisions to bid on government contracts. There is little difference between the way large and small companies have structured their organizations as a result of cost accounting standards.

To summarize, organizational structures are modified or changed if there is a perception that the effect of regulation on the company is, or will be, severe. Regardless of the regulation, or the business activity that is regulated, a company uses its administrative processes in an attempt to blunt the effects. No regulation discussed in the survey, however lightly regarded it may seem to have been by the participants, was without real impact.

Contrary to the observations of most executives interviewed for the project, the impact of most of these regulations, in terms of changes in decision-making process, was much greater for middle-sized and large companies than for smaller ones. (Even the "small" companies included are large enough to exceed the regulation's particular jurisdictional threshhold.)

In no area of regulation were the smaller companies more likely to change the authority structure than the larger ones. There are various possible explanations for this finding. For example, large companies may have a greater awareness of their responsibilities. Or the smaller companies may tend to be more centralized anyway, with the CEO already making or involved in all operational decisions. Persons speaking for large companies contend, however, that the real key may be that they consider themselves more likely targets of government regulation and investigation, and subject to the more severe demands of regulation. Thus, the larger and more complex the enterprise, the greater the demands in terms of expertise, regularity of procedures, and manpower to achieve the accurate monitoring and reporting implicit in compliance with regulation.

Chapter 3
A Corporate Civil Service

H OW HAS THE WIDESPREAD reliance on policies and procedures, the added consultation and approval, and the addition of new personnel affected the environment in which decisions are made?

One chief executive characterized the most striking change in this environment to be the development of a "counter-bureaucracy"—a cadre of specialists within the company whose knowledge, training and narrow responsibilities are characteristic of the regulators themselves. Few others agree with this rather harsh view of the new staff who, in many instances, owe their jobs to the need to achieve or monitor regulatory compliance. Most concurred, however, that regulation has the potential to create interpersonal problems.

The problems of communication between managers and internal regulators stem from their differing perspectives. An experienced line manager may tend to be flexible and pragmatic: getting the job done is the primary objective. A technical or legal employee, whose role is defined by compliance requirements and/or the avoidance of unfavorable precedents, is more concerned about *how* the job gets done. This "how" can also cause conflicts with the line manager who has been doing the work in a certain way for 20 years and sees no reason to change.

Most executives say that these kinds of problems have arisen or may arise. At the same time, many were careful to point out that conflict between legal or technical personnel and line managers had, thus far, not had a serious impact on their companies. As one company vice president with prior experience in drafting and implementing federal regulations explains: "Differences blur after a while. It started out with operations people 'set in their ways.' It was hard to get them to understand regulatory demands and consequences. In those days general managers were less likely to make ac-

18

commodations to regulatory demands than legal or technical employees. Now both groups are disgusted. The differences between the two groups is disappearing. It is hard to make a decision in some areas without considering the regulatory impact. That is just as true for line managers as it is for anyone else in the company."

Thus, although most executives do not totally agree with the "counter-bureaucracy" complaint, they do acknowledge that such tendencies exist in their companies, and that a "counter-bureaucracy" might become a problem in the future.

Concern regarding potential conflict between the managers and a "counter-bureaucracy" may account for the infrequent occurrence of individuals or committees to coordinate regulatory compliance in more than one area. Another reason for the lack of coordination between employees with compliance tasks lies in the disparate nature of regulation. Other than the common problems of dealing with state and federal bureaucracies, corporate compliance staffs may have little to share. One executive made this point in giving his company's reasons for not establishing positions or committees with the authority to coordinate regulatory activity in more than one area: "We thought about whether we needed to coordinate regulatory activity. The first problem was to decide whether this 'coordination' would involve management, or just an exchange of information. We already have a Washington office devoted to lobbying. More and more we are finding out that you have to have specialists down there to communicate with the 'other side.' The Washington office provides an umbrella for contacts and expertise. Along with that, specialists in certain areas can develop their own contacts. Beyond that, I'm not sure there is anything to be gained by contact between someone involved in energy, and another person who has responsibility for OSHA. They may have common problems in dealing with regulators, or in communicating with other parts of the company, but I am not sure there is anything to manage."

Most companies that do have committees or individuals with coordinating responsibilities agree with this observation. In almost every instance, the emphasis is the exchange of information, rather than the management of compliance activities.

As to the existence of coordinating offices, slightly more than 30 percent of the respondents (126) said they had one such person or office, 61 had two, and 13 companies have three. Only four combinations of regulatory compliance activity occurred with any frequency: (1) OSHA and environmental (38 companies); (2) equal employment opportunity and ERISA (36 companies); (3) ERISA and financial (17 companies); and (4) equal employment, ERISA, and OSHA (15 companies). In addition, eight organizations said that a person or committee had responsibility for coordinating compliance activities in *all six* regulatory areas that were part of the study. (EEOC, OSHA, ERISA, environmental, consumer and financial).

Ensuring Regulatory Compliance

Although most companies do not have a person or department that coordinates compliance activities in more than one area, a majority of companies do have at least one individual at the corporate level whose time is devoted to regulatory compliance in each of the areas examined, with the exception of consumer regulation. (In consumer regulation the percentage was 48 percent. See Table 3.) Corporate compliance personnel function largely as consultants: They furnish operations people and top management with information as to state and federal compliance standards; and they are responsible for compiling, or assisting the appropriate company officer in compiling, the reports and documentation required by state and federal regulation. In some areas, a major part of their jobs is monitoring.

A corporate-level compliance person may have any one or a combination of these three functions. It is, however, extremely rare for such an individual to be involved in the *judgmental* aspects of a particular decision, that is, he or she may inform management of waste-disposal standards at a particular location, but such an individual rarely decides whether or not the plant will be built there.

As a means of giving emphasis to this activity, most companies place full- or part-time compliance personnel at the corporate rather than division or plant level. This is especially evident in areas of regulation that affect corporate administrative concerns (EEOC, ERISA, financial). In operational areas affected by regulations, compliance staff shows up more frequently at lower levels (see Table 3).

The General Counsel's Office

Aiding and abetting compliance activity has also caused substantial increases in internal legal personnel. Nearly 85 percent of the 401 respondents (336) had a General Counsel's office in 1979. This figure was up over 20 percent from the slightly more than 60 percent (250) that said their company had such an office in 1970. All in all, 86 companies established a legal division during the 1970's.

Those organizations that already had a legal division saw this department grow far more rapidly in size than the rest of the company. Indeed, the individual who quipped: "We figure for every $100 million we gain in sales, we have to add a lawyer," was, perhaps, more right than he knew. The increase in the median size for the General Counsel's office from three to seven (233 percent) roughly paralleled the increase during the period 1970-1979 for the companies surveyed in the median sales figure (275 percent), and far outstripped the increase in the median employment totals (38 percent).

Roughly 10 percent of the respondents reported that they have General Counsel staffs exceeding 50 persons. (One company's staff numbers 400.)

Table 3: Compliance Personnel at Corporate, Division and Plant Levels

Regulatory Area	Corporate		Division		Plant	
	Number of Companies	Percent	Number of Companies	Percent	Number of Companies	Percent
EEOC.	369	92%	163	41%	148	37%
OSHA	284	71	171	43	185	46
ERISA	360	90	57	14	24	6
Environmental	242	60	154	38	163	41
Consumer	194	48	108	27	39	9
Financial	335	84	90	22	17	4

21

These include companies in virtually every business enterprise: oil, food, computers, diversified manufacturers, newspapers, chemicals, toiletries, pharmaceuticals, electrical machinery, utilities, insurance and banking. If a company is large enough, regardless of the industry, it needs a sizable legal staff.

For the most part, the legal department is limited to an advisory role and does not initiate action. The departures from this rule occur primarily in pension and consumer areas where lawyers have a special technical expertise (see Table 4).

The growth of legal offices in companies where they already exist, and the establishment of these departments where they did not, owes much to factors other than regulation. Chief among these is the increase in all aspects of litigation and the dramatically increasing cost of using outside law firms. Moreover, a higher caliber of law graduates are much more willing to accept employment with a corporation than they used to be. Thus, it is much easier than it was 10 or 20 years ago to recruit a competent, effective legal staff to deal with the increasing volume of legal problems.

Still, regulation plays a significant role in the growth, and increasing organizational importance, of the General Counsel's office. Most of the companies interviewed depend heavily on their legal office for support and assistance due to the constantly changing nature of regulatory demands. This trend was summarized by an executive of the company with the largest legal staff of any of the survey participants: "Responsibility for making decisions with potential regulatory impact is that of the line organization. The legal counsel acts for support and clarification." In addition, although companies are relying increasingly on their legal departments, they still use outside law firms. Sometimes it is the General Counsel's office that determines when that step should be taken; in other instances, company policy determines when outside law firms are to be consulted. Most often, where such policies do exist, they provide that the law firm will become involved when a regulatory problem reaches litigation.

Thus, most of the companies interviewed distinguish between policy-making and decision making. The General Counsel's office is frequently involved in the former but not the latter. The legal department also informs the corporation of legal developments that are relevant to regulatory problems, handles regulatory matters until such time as they reach litigation, and serves as a liason to the company's outside law firm. One General Counsel with a large staff described some of the difficulties his department has in keeping abreast of all of the legal aspects of its role and, at the same time, being aware of the day-to-day impact of regulatory problems on plant managers: "Our job is to inform the company that changes are needed in a certain area. After we have had our say, the corporate approach is established. We are part of a corporate team to help the plant manager comply. If things work right, day-to-day coping at the plant level should not require a lawyer's attention, and things did work right. Still, after a year I

Table 4: Involvement of General Counsel in Decision Making

Area	Number of Companies where General Counsel:			
	Initiates	Is Consulted	Approves	Is Consulted and Approves
Decision to terminate (EEOC) ...	2	84	10	2
Decision to purchase plant equipment (OSHA)...........	1	26	—	—
Selection of pension fund manager (ERISA)............	7	113	8	—
Approval of waste disposal plan (environmental).........	1	57	6	—
Product recall (consumer)	10	142	16	—
Warranty conditions (consumer).	36	108	42	2
Conditions of sale (truth in lending)	23	136	45	3
Approval of advertising copy (truth in advertising)	6	153	40	3
Decision to bid on government contract (Cost Accounting Standards Board)	3	78	3	—

discovered the legal department had suffered because it was losing awareness of day-to-day issues. For this reason I restablished ties at the plant level so we could be more aware of problems, and managers would know how we can be helpful."

Although the majority of those interviewed found the legal staff helpful, and of increasing importance in the resolution of regulatory problems, the view was by no means unanimous. Roughly one-quarter prefer, to resolve regulatory issues, where possible, by using operations employees, particularly in areas most amenable to that approach, like safety and environmental regulation. One executive, who has responsibility for environmental issues, described his approach to regulatory agencies: "We ask them is this a technical issue, or are you going to bring your lawyers? If both sides have lawyers, it makes it difficult to settle something. Everyone is being very careful as to what is said. Of course it depends on the situation, maybe you should be careful. I am not saying the presence of lawyers is good or bad, it's just different."

Choosing between the Legal Department and Law Firms

Although all the company spokespeople find it necessary to use outside law firms on occasion, this is the least common and least preferred alternative. One executive sees the use of outside lawyers as a transitional step: "We started out with operations people handling regulatory problems. Now, for the most part, we use outside law firms for difficult cases. I expect that eventually we will progress to the point where our own legal office handles most of these things."

Other than the fact that a matter has proceeded to litigation, and company policy provides that at that point outside counsel is required, corporate motives for relying on outside lawyers tend to be specialized and precise. In at least one instance the choice was not between the legal department and a law firm. One executive commented: "We use outside counsel to keep us abreast of important developments in state laws. We are a nationwide company, and we could not possibly keep up with what is going on in 50 states. In the past we used trade associations for this purpose, but now we find that we have to use law firms."

Sometimes a new and highly technical area of government regulation will require the kind of expertise that only a law firm can provide. One vice president of a large West Coast energy concern finds this to be the case with Department of Energy regulations: "Energy department regulations require a level of expertise that is hard to find outside of Washington. This has nothing to do with Washington lawyers being better lawyers. They simply get more exposure to the constantly changing regulatory climate. This is impossible to get in this area unless you are in Washington. I spend 30 to 40 percent of the time there myself. I also think that outside law firms can be helpful because they get exposure to other people's problems as well as ours."

The Use of Outside Organizations

In addition to corporate compliance/legal staff, many companies rely on consulting firms, outside legal counsel, and/or industry associations for information, advice and assistance regarding regulatory compliance. In every area but consumer regulation, more than half of the respondents say they use at least one of these three outside organizations for assistance on regulatory matters. Even with respect to consumer issues, nearly half (45 percent) say they rely on their outside legal counsel for help. (See Table 5)

Table 5: Use of Outside Organizations for Assistance in Regulated Areas

Regulatory Area	Consulting Firms		Legal Counsel		Industry Association	
	Number	Percent	Number	Percent	Number	Percent
EEOC.............	111	28%	336	84%	211	53%
OSHA	104	26	211	53	259	65
ERISA	266	66	297	74	141	35
Consumer.........	36	9	181	45	171	43
Environmental	174	43	195	49	212	53
Financial..........	211	53	239	60	161	40

Among these three different kinds of outside sources, the law firm is the most frequently utilized. A majority of the respondents use their legal counsel for EEOC, OSHA, ERISA, and financial issues, and nearly half of those queried use them for consumer and environmental problems. The law firm is the most frequently employed outside resource in four of the six regulatory areas examined, and in the others (OSHA and environmental) it is the second most common.

Next to its outside counsel, a company is most likely to rely on an industry association for assistance. In more technical operations-related areas such as OSHA and environmental regulation, industry associations are used more often than law firms.

Consulting firms place far behind the law firms and industry associations as sources companies look to for help on consumer matters, OSHA, and EEOC. Consulting firms have, however, carved a niche for themselves in financial regulation and in a related area (ERISA). In addition, a substantial number of companies use consulting organizations for environmental issues (43 percent), though the figure is lower than the percentages that use law firms or industry associations.

Chapter 4
Decision Making: The Current Cast

WHEN ASKED TO DESCRIBE how regulation has affected the decision-making process in their organization, many company representatives say, "By and large the same persons still have the responsibility, but we try to give them all the help that we can." "Help" in this context means policy directives, staff to lend counsel and interpret both policy and directives, and in a large number of cases, the use of law firms, consultants and industrial associations for additional assistance. In short, a host of people— both internal and external—are now involved. This raises questions as to who really does make decisions in areas covered by regulation.

Power to Act?

One way of analyzing this problem is to consider how a baseball team functions in different situations. When the pressure is on—for example, the bases are loaded, the team is ahead by one run, there are two outs in the bottom of the ninth, and the World Series rides on the next pitch, other players may visit the pitcher's box, and the catcher will look to the bench for a decision from the manager as to what the pitcher should do. This is one extreme in a continuum where the key factor is risk. At the other extreme, if by the bottom of the ninth the pitcher has thrown a no-hitter, and the team is already ahead ten runs, there is little risk, so the pitcher can throw any kind of pitch he wants. Most management decisions occur at a point somewhere toward the middle of this risk continuum. The degree to which the decision occupies a point in the direction of the first example determines, in large measure, the extent to which additional players, and even the manager, may become involved in the pitcher's decision as to what kind of pitch to throw; or, even, whether that *particular* pitcher is the person most qualified to pitch to the batter.

In the absence of extraordinary circumstances, the issue of who has ultimate authority or responsibility simply does not arise. How the players go about doing their job is not an issue of authority at all: it depends on (1) the rules of baseball; (2) the policies and internal rules, expressed and implied, of the team; and (3) the respect and working relationships they have with one another.

Similarly in business, decisions under usual circumstances do not require much in the way of consultation, review, and/or approval. When the bases are empty and the team is ten runs ahead, most teams, indeed most companies, act pretty much alike; when the bases are loaded each acts differently, and in its own way. The regulatory environment has the effect of transforming certain routine business actions (like the termination of an employee) into a "bases loaded" situation.

The foregoing analogy demonstrates that companies, for the most part, place decisions with regulatory implications on a reasonably high level with respect to the risk continuum. Nonetheless, plant-level personnel continue to have important responsibilities for initiating and deciding what is to be done in regulatory areas where local conditions are of key importance—EEOC, OSHA, and environmental—but they are often required to consult other individuals or policy regulations. On the other hand, action regarding pension management is initiated at the corporate level. Actions regarding consumer issues and bidding on government contracts may begin at the corporate or divisional level, depending on how the company is organized. (See Table 6.)

The Plant Executive

To the extent that he or she is involved in the process, the role of the plant manager, or plant functional executive, is most often to decide what is to be

Table 6: Level at which Decisions Are Initiated[1]

Decision	Corporate Level Number	Corporate Level Percent	Divisional Level Number	Divisional Level Percent	Plant Level Number	Plant Level Percent
To terminate minority female employee	54	13%	33	8%	316	78%
To purchase equipment . . .	52	13	65	16	291	71
Choice of fund manager . . .	301	95	12	4	7	2
Waste disposal plan	81	21	55	15	242	64
Product recall.	120	44	106	39	49	18
Terms of warranty	116	48	104	43	24	10
Terms or condition of sale .	133	49	105	39	31	12
Advertising copy	155	50	119	39	35	11
Whether or not to bid on government contract .	71	31	117	52	39	17

[1]In some cases, the number of individuals having the authority to initiate or decide what *is* to be done, exceeds the total number of questionnaires. This suggests that in some companies more than one person has that authority.

done and to initiate action. Initiation of action by plant executives is most common in employee-oriented areas such as EEOC and OSHA, and on environmental issues that are often local in their focus.

The evidence of continued authority for plant executives in these areas (which had been traditionally within their purview) is impressive. Despite regulatory pressures, the need for familiarity with local conditions, with equal employment opportunity, safety and environmental issues, is such that plant managers and functional officers continue to formulate responses to these kinds of problems (see Table 7). In interviews, most executives note that the only real change in this regard is that now a plant manager has to know about regulation in addition to everything else.

The Divisional Executive

The role of the divisional executive in decisions that invite regulatory scrutiny is far more varied than that of plant or corporate managers.

Where the decision involves employee-oriented issues, for example EEOC and OSHA, the divisional role tends to be one of review and approval of action initiated at the plant level. This is also true of environmental questions which, in many companies, have a strong regional emphasis.

On the other hand, in consumer areas where divisional responsibilities for sales and marketing plans are often very great, the division frequently has the responsibility for initiating action and deciding what is to be done. Bidding on government contracts under Cost Accounting Standards Board regulations is one activity in which the divisional role is fairly evenly divided

Table 7: Involvement of Operating Managers and Lower-Level Executives in Decision Making

Area	Number of Companies where:		
	Initiates and Decides	Is Consulted	Approves Final Decision
Decision to terminate (EEOC)	316	90	95
Decision to purchase plant equipment (OSHA)	291	95	38
Selection of fund manager (ERISA)	7	2	4
Development of waste disposal plan (environmental)	242	96	32
Product recall (consumer)	49	42	4
Warranty conditions (consumer)	24	15	2
Conditions of sale (Truth in Lending)	31	16	5
Approval of advertising copy (Truth in Advertising)	35	13	6
Decision to bid on government contract (Cost Accounting Standards Board)	39	14	5

Table 8: Involvement of Divisional Executives in Decision Making

Area	Number of Companies where:		
	Initiates and Decides	Is Consulted	Approves Final Decision
Decision to terminate (EEOC).	33	116	121
Decision to purchase plant equipment (OSHA).	65	141	189
Selection of fund manager (ERISA)	12	9	5
Development of waste disposal plan (environmental)	55	129	157
Product recall (consumer).	106	78	81
Warranty conditions (consumer)	104	53	88
Conditions of sale (Truth in Lending). . .	105	43	95
Approval of advertising copy (Truth in Advertising).	119	56	104
Decision to bid on government contract (Cost Accounting Standards Board) .	121	51	111

between initiation and approval. The largest number of respondents say the division's function is to initiate action. This figure is higher than the number saying that either the corporate or plant level is responsible for the initial recommendation as to whether or not to bid on a government contract. Contract bidding, in fact, is the one area in which more companies initiate action at the divisional than at the plant or corporate levels.

The variety of divisional responsibilities reflects the many different kinds of companies that participated in the study, and the varying degrees of responsibility assigned to the divisions (see Table 8). The divisional pattern does, however, reinforce one observation: The center of gravity for employment and environmental problems is local, while the locus of authority for consumer issues is national. Resolution of the first group of questions requires flexibility in response to local conditions, while resolving consumer issues (this is also true of pension questions) demands a coherent and uniform corporate approach.

The Corporate Executive

Corporate functional executives become involved in decisions with regulatory import in fulfilling one of two roles in company organization. In the first role, as staff for the entire organization, the corporate executive participates in decision making primarily by giving advice.

The second approach is to act as the arm of the chief executive in a specialized area. In this particular capacity, the corporate executive may have the responsibility for initiating or deciding what is to be done, or for approving final decisions with regulatory implications.

Survey data indicate that, with the exception of ERISA, the primary, but not exclusive, role of corporate management is the consultative one. (See Table 9.) This is not true with ERISA because, for the most part, both initiation and consultation take place at the corporate level in pension-related decisions. In decisions where local conditions are germane to sound conclusions, the corporate role recedes to one of consultation, and, in some cases, approval— but rarely initiation. This is true for EEOC, OSHA and environmental issues.

With respect to consumer problems, there is greater variation in the nature of the corporate role. Again, the most frequent involvement is as a consultant. The data also reflect, however, that participating companies are just as likely to decide what is to be done with respect to consumer issues at the corporate as at the divisional level, and, of course, initiation at the plant level is rare for decisions on consumer-related issues.

Again, the reason for corporate and divisional responsibility in consumer questions lies in the nature of these problems. Warranty conditions, product recall, advertising copy, and sales terms all involve the formulation of policies that require at least a divisional and, frequently, a corporate perspective.

With government contract bidding, respondents indicate that the division most often takes the lead in initiating and deciding what is to be done, and the most frequently cited corporate activity is consultation. Still, in a substantial minority of cases, initial action is taken at the corporate level, and in a much larger number of companies final authorization is required from a corporate department.

The CEO's Role

With the exception of important decisions in pension funding, any participation by the CEO in decisions with regulatory impact was rare. Where the CEO is involved in decision making the role is almost exclusively one of review and approval. (See Table 10.)

Nonetheless, interviews reveal that while the CEO's involvement in *actual* decisions is usually minimal, it is invariably the CEO who determines the whole tone and environment in which decisions are made. If the boss's attitude is one of defiance, or passive compliance, lower level personnel may continue to have broad discretion in decisions with potential regulatory impact. If, however, the CEO sets guidelines as to how compliance is to be achieved or, in even more extreme cases, chooses to exercise functional control over decisions with regulatory impact, it is a different story. In those instances, increasingly common in the experience of those interviewed, it is still unusual for the CEO to become directly involved, but corporate departments become active in the execution of policy, which has been set from the top.

Moreover, it appears that potential regulatory exposure is not the cause,

Table 9: Involvement of Corporate Executives in Decision Making

| | Number of Companies where: | | |
Area	Initiates and Decides	Is Consulted	Approves Final Decision
Decision to terminate (EEOC).........	54	264	123
Decision to purchase plant equipment (OSHA)........................	52	294	209
Selection of fund manager (ERISA)	301	328	302
Development of waste disposal plan (environmental)	81	246	192
Product recall (consumer)............	120	326	196
Warranty conditions (consumer)	116	211	143
Conditions of sale (Truth in Lending)...	133	260	175
Approval of advertising copy (Truth in Advertising)..............	155	253	195
Decision to bid on government contract (Cost Accounting Standards Board) .	71	237	116

Table 10: Involvement of the CEO in Decision Making

| | Number of Companies where: | | | |
Area	Initiates	Is Consulted	Approves	Is Consulted and Approves
Decision to terminate (EEOC)	2	10	24	—
Decision to purchase plant equipment (OSHA)............	1	12	139	3
Selection of fund manager (ERISA).	28	35	235	7
Development of waste disposal plan (environmental)...........	2	10	118	3
Product recall (consumer)	6	17	144	3
Warranty conditions (consumer)...	5	8	69	—
Conditions of sale (Truth in Lending)..................	3	10	72	2
Approval of advertising copy (Truth in Advertising)...........	1	15	3	—
Decision to bid on government contract (Cost Accounting Standards Board)	5	13	77	1

in most instances, of the direct involvement of the CEO. The major factor in the need to seek the approval of the CEO is usually *cost*. Thus, purchases of plant equipment, waste disposal plans, and product recall programs frequently require the CEO's approval, while actions that may result in EEOC exposure do not. It is not a measure of the severity of the regulatory body's effect on the company; most organizations view the impact of EEOC legislation as being much more severe than consumer or safety regulation.

The important criterion, then, in getting the CEO's attention is the initial *actual,* not the *potential,* cost. New plant equipment can be expensive, as is the decision to cease manufacturing, or to recall a product (for any reason), and that is why such actions require the approval of top management. Interviews with executives confirm, for example, that the issue on plant equipment purchases is frequently the dollar amount of the purchase, and not vulnerability to OSHA regulation.

Chapter 5

Regulation: Assessing the Severity of the Impact

W HAT DO ALL these changes add up to in terms of severity of effect on the way a company does business? When given an opportunity to characterize the degree of impact of the various regulatory changes chosen by The Conference Board as the subject of this study, the dominant view is that the effect has been moderate rather than severe. This view is further buttressed by the degree of organizational change reported in answers to specific questions. (See Table 11.)

Two areas of regulation—EEOC and environmental protection—were singled out as being far more significant than the others—OSHA, ERISA, consumer and financial. This general outlook is confirmed by evidence of transfers of *actual* authority for decision making—in the EEOC area, well over half the participating companies did so. With respect to certain environmental issues, nearly half the companies reported upward shifts in authority.

This view of major federal regulatory developments of the last decade is hard to square with the outrage that business has expressed on the subject of regulation. There are two possible reasons why this position is not confirmed by the survey data.

First, the whole is greater than the sum of its parts. When asked for an opinion on a given piece of regulation the answer is likely to be that its effect has been moderate. Taken as a whole, however, the demands of a climate that is heavily regulated may be severe.

Secondly, for many businesses the regulation with the most severe effects was not the landmark legislation, like equal employment and environmental protection, which comes to mind when the subject is raised, and which The Conference Board used in developing this study. For a good number of companies, the regulatory nightmare has been due to regulation of a more particular nature—for example, local bottle disposal ordinances, state strip-mining acts, and obscure foreign-trade rulings. In large measure this regulatory activity is unnoticed by the public, but it has, in many instances,

Table 11: Severity of Impact of Major 1970's Regulatory Legislation

Legislation	Number of Companies Responding:				
	Severe	Moderate	Minimal	No Impact	Total
EEOC	131	201	59	4	395
OSHA	82	209	88	12	391
ERISA..........	61	190	122	19	392
Environment	158	109	77	42	386
Consumer	40	110	139	71	360
Financial	92	197	70	25	384

the power of life and death over the business activities it affects. Much of it, as already mentioned, is local in nature, and all of it is specialized in its focus.

In a sense, then, the regulatory climate has two tiers. The first tier consists of those regulations that are designed to effect the broad social and political objectives to which most of the population is deeply committed—social justice, clean air and water, a safe workplace, and a secure pension.

There is, however, a second tier of regulation to which the public is perhaps less committed, and of which it is most certainly less aware. This second tier may well be the product of the energies generated by the first, but its objectives are not general—social or political—they are specific and their impact is almost purely economic. Conversations with executives show that, in large measure, this is the "regulation" that is so often complained of. There may, indeed, be a relationship between these so-called broad- and the second more narrow-gauged regulations—for example, general concern for the environment, which gave rise to clean air and water acts, also spawned the "bottle laws," that are narrower in their focus but more severe in the effect they have on those businesses that are subject to them. The fact remains that the effect of the regulation which has had a substantial impact on American life is perceived as moderate, in large measure because of attempts by business to deal with these kinds of problems prior to regulation (see Table 2). Yet most business-people, when asked, would probably characterize the regulatory climate as a far more severe problem.

Exceptions to this overall perception of a moderate impact exist on the basis of industry, number of employees, and/or sales volume. What emerges is a picture of regulation as a phenomenon with widely varying effects depending on the regulation, the industry, the number of employees, and the sales volume.

Regulatory Impact by Industry

As previously noted, EEOC and environmental regulation are the only areas whose impact was deemed severe by a third or more respondents.

Nonetheless, when the responses are broken down by industrial groups there are considerable differences. As Tables 12 and 13 show, the impact of EEOC regulation is deemed less significant by manufacturers than by utilities and financial institutions. More predictable has been the greater impact of environmental legislation on manufacturers and utilities than on banks and insurance companies.

Most other industry-based distinctions conform to expectation and logic. Roughly three-fifths of all manufacturers and utilities find the effects of OSHA to be moderate. Not surprisingly, nearly seven out of ten financial institutions viewed the effects of safety and health legislation as minimal.

Similarly, ERISA provokes a fairly uniform response with slightly more than half of all respondents in manufacturing, utilities and retail trade characterizing its effects as moderate. The one exception is the financial institutions—almost 40 percent say ERISA's effect on their company is severe, and another 30 percent say it is moderate.

Commenting on ERISA, an insurance company executive alluded to the greater impact of ERISA on financial institutions: "As an employer the requirements of ERISA are fairly easily understood, as a pension writer and administrator we have great difficulty in knowing what our responsibilites are due to the vagaries of the preemption provision of the law. We simply do not know which state laws have been preempted and which have not. Our customers have an interest in pension uniformity, which is consistent with a broad interpretation of the preemption provision, while the National Association of Insurance Commissioners wants a narrow interpretation which preempts state law as little as possible. We're caught between the two and we get very little guidance from the law, which is poorly drafted."

Financial regulation is another area where the dominant response is consistent throughout various industry groups; over half of all manufacturers, utilities and retail establishments view its effect as moderate. The exception, again, is the financial institution. Not surprisingly, nearly 40 percent of them feel that financial regulation had a severe impact on the company.

The broadest disagreement among industry groups concerns the effect of consumer regulation. The largest number of companies characterized the impact as minimal, or not present at all. (Over six out of ten of the utilities checked the "no impact" category). Among financial institutions, more companies checked either severe, or no impact, than moderate (see Table 14).

Regulatory Impact by Size of Company

In speaking with executives, the dominant impression is that regulation hurts small business the most. The consensus among those interviewed is that, assuming jurisdictional minima with respect to the size of the company, larger companies, by virtue of superior resources, are better equipped to deal with regulatory problems than smaller organizations. The minority

Table 12: Impact of EEOC, by Industrial Group

Type of Business	Impact Evaluation:								
	Severe		Moderate		Minimal		None		Total
	Number	Percent[a]	Number	Percent[a]	Number	Percent[a]	Number	Percent[a]	
Manufacturing[1]	83	28%	153	52%	52	18%	4	1%	292
Utilities	15	44	17	50	2	6	—	—	34
Financial	30	53	26	46	1	2	—	—	57
Retail	3	25	5	42	4	33	—	—	12

[1]Includes one mining and six construction companies.

[a]Percentages do not add to 100 because of rounding.

Table 13: Impact of Environmental Legislation, by Industrial Group

Type of Business	Impact Evaluation:								
	Severe		Moderate		Minimal		None		Total
	Number	Percent[a]	Number	Percent[a]	Number	Percent[a]	Number	Percent[a]	
Manufacturing[1]	128	44%	95	33%	54	19%	12	4%	289
Utilities	28	82	4	12	2	6	—	—	34
Financial	—	—	5	10	18	35	29	56	52
Retail	2	18	5	46	3	27	1	9	11

[1]Includes one mining and six construction companies.

[a]Percentages do not add to 100 because of rounding.

view is summarized by an executive of a large company: "The organizational impact on large companies is greater. We attract more attention. In dollars we are required to spend more money. Our unit costs are even higher for this reason."

Still, when company spokesmen are asked to describe the organizational effects of regulation on their *own* companies, as opposed to their *perception* of its effects on large and small organizations, the picture is far more diverse and variegated. It appears that size, as a determinant of regulatory impact, varies in significance depending upon the area of regulation. In addition, the definition of "size" itself is important. (With EEOC regulation, for example, size as determined by employee population is a less powerful variable than size defined by annual sales.)

Equal Employment Opportunity Commission

When companies are grouped by size according to the number of persons employed, there is little difference between the impact on small and large companies. A slightly different picture emerges when comparing companies with annual sales above and below the $250 million figure. In this instance, more of the larger companies consider the effect of EEOC regulation to be "severe" or "moderate" than is the case with the smaller organizations. (See Table 15.)

These data are somewhat at odds with the observations of those interviewed who find that larger companies were more likely to be the focus of EEOC attention. While that may, in fact, be the case, it is apparent that smaller businesses *perceive* the impact to be as severe as do larger employers.

Occupational Safety and Health Administration

Whether the criterion for size is work force or sales, more smaller than larger companies report difficulty. More than 80 percent of the smaller companies in both the work force and sales categories (under 2,500 employees, $250 million annual sales) say that OSHA has had a severe or moderate effect on their company, while roughly 70 percent of the larger companies are of that opinion. Moreover, one-fourth of the small companies consider the effect of OSHA to be severe while only one-fifth of the large companies hold this view.

Employee Retirement Income Security Act

Roughly two-thirds of all the respondents feel that the effect of ERISA on their company is severe or moderate. Whether the companies are categorized by annual sales, or size of work force the difference between large and small companies is slight.

Interviews with executives tell a slightly different story. Since one of the

Table 14: Impact of Consumer Regulation, by Industry Group

Type of Business	Impact Evaluation:								
	Severe		Moderate		Minimal		None		Total
	Number	Percent[a]	Number	Percent	Number	Percent	Number	Percent	
Manufacturing[1]............	27	10%	94	34%	117	42%	40	14%	278
Utilities................	—	—	4	17	5	22	14	61	23
Financial...............	9	19	6	13	15	32	17	36	47
Retail..............	4	33	6	50	2	17	—	—	12

[1]Includes one mining and six construction companies.

Table 15: Impact of EEOC Regulation, by Company Size

Type of Business	Impact Evaluation:								
	Severe		Moderate		Minimal		None		Total
	Number	Percent	Number	Percent	Number	Percent	Number	Percent	
Number of Employees									
under 2500............	31	34	50	54	10	11	1	1	92
over 2500............	99	33	150	50	47	16	3	1	299
Annual Sales									
under $250 million	25	27	45	49	20	22	2	2	92
over $250 million...........	94	34	142	52	37	13	1	▼1	274

most frequent complaints against ERISA is its reporting requirements to plan beneficiaries, companies with a large number of employees, in this view, are likely to be more seriously affected.

Environmental Protection

Environmental regulation is the area in which the most substantial differences appear in effects between smaller and larger companies. But here the difference becomes meaningful only when companies with over 10,000 employees, or over $1 billion in sales (there were 137 companies in the former category and 134 in the latter), are compared with the rest of the sample. Roughly half of the respondents in the larger companies (defined either way) viewed the effect of environmental regulation to be *severe,* while slightly more than one-third of the smaller companies are of that opinion. Complementing these survey data was the observation of one executive: "I'm not sure that doubling your size doubles your problems, but the government certainly gets more for its surveillance dollar in focusing on large companies."

Obviously, this is especially true in environmental regulation where a large company's failure to comply with the law may have a more serious effect than a small company's dereliction. Greater likelihood of surveillance, however, is only one facet of the more severe effect of environmental regulation on larger companies. One must assume that all companies, large and small, have established compliance with environmental regulations as a corporate objective. Clearly, larger companies consider the organizational impact of the effort to achieve the objective to be greater than do smaller companies.

Consumer Protection

There is little difference between large and small companies as to the organizational impact of consumer regulation. Depending on whether company size is determined by work force or annual sales (again, using $250 million in annual sales, or 2,500 employees as a break point), the number of those answering "severe" or "moderate" varies only 3 percentage points— from 40 to 43 percent. Consumer regulation is also the only major area of regulation examined by The Conference Board in which a majority of the respondents do not consider the impact on the company to be "severe" or "moderate."

Financial Regulation

With financial regulation, the larger the company—regardless of whether employees or sales is used as an index—the more likely the company is to report that financial regulation has had a "moderate" impact. Roughly 60 percent of the very large companies (over 10,000 employees or over $1

Deregulation: The Experience of United Airlines

Are regulation and deregulation different sides of the same coin? In some sense yes; and in some sense no.

The experience of United Airlines demonstrates that the lifting of regulatory burdens also requires adjustment, and that these demands are not so very different from those imposed by the need to achieve some sort of accommodation with the regulatory environment. "Deregulation in our case has caused us to move toward a more centralized decision-making process at higher levels in the organization," states Perry E. Brown, Director of Organization Planning, United Airlines.

Deregulation, in Brown's estimation, has created something of a "dilemma." He states: "On the one hand, it is important that we have a coherent pricing strategy. Scheduling also requires companywide coordination. This suggests centralization. But certain decentralizing tendencies remain: The advantage of deregulation is that we are now able to respond quickly to changes in local markets. You cannot do this, however, without knowledge of the markets. Each area has its own special needs and preferences. We also have different competitors in different regions, so we have to have accurate and timely inputs from people thoroughly familiar with local conditions.

Reminiscing about United's adjustment to various forms of regulation in areas other than rates and routes, Brown noted that there were some similarities and some differences: "Because we were a decentralized organization to begin with, we had to come up with certain devices to be sure that we were complying with regulatory requirements. The development of corporate affirmative action plans, for example, was, and remains, centralized. This is also true with pensions. We have a committee overseeing pension reform. Safety and health programs are the responsibility of central staff groups. Regulation and deregulation have given rise to the same centralizing

billion in sales) say financial regulation has had a "moderate" effect. By the same token, the smaller the company (under 2,500 employees or under $250 million in sales), the more likely the respondent was to check "minimal" or "no impact." In each category, one third said that financial regulation had minimal or no impact.

Regulatory Impact: What Are the Problems?

How does the regulatory climate affect the development of company priorities, and strategies, and the means of achieving them? Is rapid growth an effective antidote to all regulatory problems, or does it create additional difficulties that are not present in low growth, or no growth environments? Has regulation focused attention on previously ignored areas that should tendencies, but with these types of regulation we have not found the same need for strong regional or local input."

Prior to deregulation, certain economic factors—for example, higher fuel prices—were exerting pressure toward centralization on United Airlines' basically decentralized organizational structure. While deregulation has not reversed this trend, Brown sees a requirement for a greater focus on the marketplace: "In the past, economic factors worked together to put the emphasis on cost effectiveness. As higher costs cut more into profit margins, tendencies toward centralization became greater. In those days we had little choice but to focus on costs. We could not change our rates, offer special services, or compete aggressively in new markets without elaborate and time-consuming red tape, and oftentimes we could not do it at all. Most of the ball game was cost controls. Now, deregulation has forced us to compete: we have the flexibility on the revenue side and that means more attention to regional and local marketing opportunities. Local inputs can be rather critical under these circumstances. Cost effectiveness is still extremely important, and probably even more so, but now there is more of a balance in emphasis between costs and revenues."

The staffing implications of deregulation have not been especially traumatic. There has been some shifting of staff from field organizations to headquarters. "The CAB group," said Brown, "was small to begin with. It is now shrinking. However, international rates continue to be regulated. The Department of Justice will continue to monitor our rate structure to protect the public and competitors from predatory rates, and we have to be careful with antitust, so we are not entirely free of regulatory issues. We also need liaison work with small communities. We can use some of those people for these kinds of problems, and reassigment and attrition will take care of the rest."

have received more attention in the past? Executives were asked to comment on these aspects of regulation's impact on their companies. Once again, the dominant view was one of moderate effect—regulation has been an important influence, but it has not precipitated severe changes.

Slower Decision-making Process

Regardless of how company size is defined (by employees or by sales), most of the respondents (88 percent) feel that increased regulation has resulted in administrative changes that cause the decision-making process to operate at a "slower pace." In practice, "slower" often appears to mean "more complicated." One executive summarized this view:

"We continue to use the same people. We just add more bodies due to the demands for overwhelming amounts of data. A company like ours has a choice—either you divert management from its essential tasks or you hire specialists. We opt for specialists in most cases. We expect managers to manage the business and call specialists when we need them."

The slower pace or more cumbersome procedures are not necessarily viewed as problems. Another respondent notes that slower procedures have sometimes produced better results, saving time in the long run: "It may take more time to develop a clean manufacturing process, but once you have it, you can put it anywhere. If you have a dirty plant, there are fewer options."

Thus, although there is agreement that a "slower pace of decision making" results from regulation, this effect does not appear to be viewed with alarm, and, in a few cases, is even welcomed.

Development of Good Managers

What about the effect of regulation on the development of managerial talent? Does the need for constant review and approval of decisions, or, in some cases, the absence of decision-making freedom due to policy or legal constraints, hinder the development of self-reliant individuals who can make decisions and take responsibility for them?

Three out of four respondents do not feel that constraints imposed by regulation impede the training of managers. (Among companies with more than 10,000 employees, or $1 billion in sales, the figure was even higher—well over 80 percent.) Most of those who were interviewed agree with that assessment.

In private conversations executives saw regulatory constraints simply as additional material the promising manager has to integrate. As one executive noted:

"We have to make young managers aware of issues. But once we do, a successful manager will deal with regulatory issues just as he or she manages interest rate problems. If someone makes a dumb decision on EPA, it is the same as any other kind of dumb decision. A manager is responsible for whatever advice is accepted or ignored."

Other executives go even further and find positive effects of regulation on managerial development. One observes: "It is certainly true that lower- and middle-echelon people must now put together more detailed analyses of operations. This requirement may have a broadening or developmental effect on them. It can pay off in the future with greater skills." Another individual noted: "Regulation may actually be helpful to an aggressive young person, in giving them more of an opportunity to show what he or she can do."

Both of the executives quoted, however, are less sanguine as to the effects of regulation on appraisal and promotion procedures. One of them said:

"Regulation complicates the results of the management process. Ability to deal with the regulatory environment has to be recognized and quantified. It has been difficult for us, but we can do it. It has complicated our system, but it has not destroyed it. The results have been predictable. The good people are still the good people, and the turkeys are still turkeys. High achievers are more easily identified; the chasms between the good and the bad are wider."

The second executive found regulation to be even more of a problem in the appraisal process: "These externalities tend to make it more difficult to fix responsibility. It is not that the individual does a cop-out, it is more a question of the necessary diffusion of responsibility and accountability."

Regulation and Overseas Competition

Approximately three out of five respondents feel that regulation impairs their company's ability to compete in domestic markets against foreign competitors. Among larger companies, the percentage is even higher—over two-thirds of the 127 companies employing more than 10,000 persons said regulation hurts them against foreign competitors. Since relatively few utilities and retail establishments responded to this question, the sample respondents were primarily manufacturers and financial institutions. That manufacturers find regulation a hindrance is no news, a bit more unexpected is that so many financial institutions have similar problems existing from regulation (Table 16).

One vice president of a large western bank observes that foreign competition is a fact of life for many banks: "It depends on who you talk to, money center banks, regional banks, any big bank would say that regulation hurts them against foreign competition. There isn't anyone who would disagree with that. In New York, foreign banks have 45 percent of the commerical loan market; on the West Coast the figure is about 30 percent. On the other hand, most banks are small local 'mom and pop' outfits that have no foreign competition."

Even though three out of five manufacturers said regulation hurt them in domestic markets against foreign competitors, it is also worth remembering

Table 16: Impact of Regulation on Ability to Compete Domestically Against Foreign Competition

Type of Business	Hindrance		No Impact		
	Number	Percent	Number	Percent	Total
Manufacturing.	173	62%	108	38%	281
Financial	20	49	21	51	41
Total.	193	60	129	40	322

that two out of five companies were not of that opinion. One executive from a heavy manufacturing company expresses a minority view on this issue: "Regulation has not been a major factor in increasing costs. We are still competitive against foreign companies because of cheaper energy."

Changing Priorities

Legislators, and the public that elected them, would like to believe that laws and regulations force companies to pay attention to previously overlooked societal problems. While a significant minority (38 percent) of the companies responding share this opinion, the majority disagree. This is especially evident among very large companies (more than $5 billion in sales). Less than one-third of these larger organizations say that regulation helped to focus attention on problems that company management was not addressing at the time the legislation was passed.

Conversations with executives shed light on this division of opinion. All of those interviewed felt that much current regulation is directed at achieving important objectives. Regulation with broadly defined social goals such as EEOC and environmental legislation were widely supported by most of those interviewed. By the same token, little or no support could be found for certain types and agencies of economic regulation, for example, the Department of Energy and the Council on Wage and Price Stability. Thus, in some cases the validity of many regulatory objectives was questioned, while in others the issue was the effectiveness of government implementation. Still another factor was the effectiveness with which the company had dealt with the problem prior to regulation. In this regard, for example, many executives felt that equal opportunity or environmental legislation was necessary for *other* companies; they did not feel it was necessary for *their* company.

One test of whether or not a company had a long-standing commitment to resolution of certain problems is the previously referred to presence or absence of internal administrative or policy regulation prior to the advent of legislation (Table 2). These internal regulations take a variety of forms, but their objective is the same as that of government regulation: to promote and achieve important objectives—for example, equal employment, a safe work place, or a secure pension—and to measure the extent to which the company is accomplishing those objectives.

Although it appears obvious that companies that had no previous policies in certain areas would feel that regulation had helped them to focus on important problems, this proved to be the case only with EEOC and OSHA. (See Table 17.) The small, or nonexistent, differences between companies with prior constraints and companies that did not have them in areas such as pension administration, advertising and cost accounting can be explained by the relatively well-established, long-standing concern of business with these subjects. The most difficult findings to explain are the environmental

Table 17: Increased Sensitivity of Companies to Regulatory Areas

| Regulation | Had Internal Guidelines Prior to Regulation | | | | No Guidelines Prior to Regulation | | | |
| | Now Pay More Attention to Issues | | No Change | | Now Pay More Attention to Issues | | No Change | |
	Number	Percent	Number	Percent	Number	Percent	Number	Percent
EEOC.	75	34%	147	66%	66	43%	87	57%
OSHA	80	35	148	65	53	45	66	55
ERISA	98	37	170	63	35	39	55	61
Air/Water Pollution	80	39	124	61	41	37	70	63
Consumer Product Safety	68	37	116	63	23	35	42	65
Magnuson-Moss FTC Improvement (warrants) . . .	69	39	110	61	20	32	42	68
Truth in Lending.	80	40	120	60	26	33	54	68
Truth in Advertising	90	37	151	63	36	38	59	62
Cost Accounting Standards.	62	38	102	62	31	36	55	64

and consumer areas. A larger percentage of those companies that had restrictions *prior* to regulation actually said regulation was beneficial in requiring attention to overlooked problems than those companies that had not previously had internal policies on these issues. This response may well be motivated by industry rather than company considerations. Companies are relieved to see that their competition is now required by law to take those measures they felt were necessary all along.

One executive in a large company with a long history of concern about consumer issues supplied a useful perspective in this regard: "Regulation eliminates elements of risk which top management takes in doing something desirable in the consumer area that will cost money. Even top management is not immune; they have to worry about shareholders. If both you and your competitors are forced to do it by regulation, that relieves the pressure." In other words, companies with a history of careful practice in environmental and consumer problems may actually find regulation helpful not because it focuses the attention of their organization on important issues, but because it forces their competitors to do so, and, in the process, eliminates whatever competitive advantage the rival business may have had in the past.

Whatever their company's view on various forms of regulation, many executives feel that the regulatory environment has helped them to get a hearing for programs and ideas that they consider important. One respondent summarized this view:

"It is a question of degree. I do not think the company overlooked these areas in the past, but they have escalated in importance. It is a question of priorities; it has heightened everyone's interest and encouraged employees to speak out more freely than in the past. This is consistent with what our whole society is doing. Individual rights, such as privacy, are important. The person is getting the attention; the system is suspect. Regulation is a manifestation of changing attitudes, not the cause of them."

Another individual acknowledged that the regulatory environment had helped him to develop a constituency for some of his ideas, but he was much less sanguine about the general climate of opinion within the company and more blunt about the coercive effects of regulation:

"We always want to avoid being the bad guys. Many of us felt the company had certain responsibilities. My personal experience in many of these areas was resistence. Management warmed up as they had regulation forced on them. Some guys turned into screaming liberals because it was the smart thing to do."

Regulation and Growth

Whether measured by a larger work force or a higher annual sales volume, the 1970's was a decade of rapid growth for many companies (see

Table 18: Growth Patterns of Survey Respondents: 1970 to 1979

	Number of Companies
Employee Growth (384 Companies Responding)	
No Growth	77
1—19%	83
20—39%	65
40—79%	82
Above 80%	77
Sales Growth (363 Companies Responding)	
0— 99%	60
100—199%	112
200—299%	109
Over 300%	82

Table 18). The responses show how the regulatory climate in general, and certain types of regulation in particular, have had differing effects on companies, depending on whether the organization achieved no growth, slow growth, average or high growth.

In general, a growing company is slightly less likely to regard the effects of the regulation in the survey (EEOC, OSHA, ERISA, environmental, consumer, and financial) as severe. Exceptions to this rule are consumer regulation where high-growth companies reported a slightly heavier impact, and— most particularly—financial regulation, where high-growth companies complain of a more severe burden.

Whether a company's growth is measured by a larger work force, or increased sales (in some cases, of course, it was both), there was a strong correlation between growth and reports of the severe impact of financial regulation. For no-growth and low-growth companies, less than 20 percent considered the effect of financial regulation to be severe. For high-growth organizations (those 81 companies whose annual sales had risen more than 300 percent during the last decade) the figure was 37 percent. The figure of 37 percent exceeds the percentage of companies in the high sales-growth group that reported that environmental regulation had a severe effect on their company and was 7 points higher than the percentage of those complaining that EEOC legislation had had a severe effect. In sum, for high-growth companies financial regulation has proven to be as much of a worry as more highly visible environmental and EEOC legislation.

When asked if he thought regulation had a more severe effect on high-growth companies, one executive replied: "Any problem a high-growth company faces is likely to be less severe; volume covers a lot of sins." Other executives, who concurred with this view, pointed out that a rapidly growing company has a greater capacity to comply with government demands, particularly with respect to equal employment opportunity.

In general, the survey data support this executive's hypothesis with respect to high-growth companies. High-growth organizations were just as likely as slower growth companies to feel that regulation forces business to operate at a slower pace, but they were less likely to think that regulation affected their abilities to develop good managers and to compete in domestic markets against foreign competition. The 81 companies whose sales increased more than 300 percent during the 1970's were also less likely than the 280 companies that grew at a slower pace (28 percent) to agree with the statement that regulation had forced the company to pay attention to important problems. (Forty-three percent of these organizations agreed with this view.) If grouped by growth in size of work force, however, there was no significant difference in the response of high-growth and low-growth companies.

When interviewed, executives of high-growth companies often had their own special sets of concerns. An assistant to the president of one of the fastest growing companies in the United States noted: "The traditional areas of governmental regulation which are the subject of your study have less organizational impact on us than on other companies. Our real problem has been with the government's export regulations. We do not know where to invest our money. One minute the government says 'sell to the Eastern Bloc'; the next minute they pass a regulation that says we can no longer do it. This tends to make you more staid in your sales program."

Another executive of a fast growing energy company also feels the major regulatory areas selected for the study were less important than those specialized regulations affecting his own industry. He states: "Regulation helps to maintain the position of the persons who are in the business at the time it is initiated. As a result, a lot of regulation is anticompetitive, and does not favor high-growth companies or industries."

Most executives of fast growing companies would agree with the individual who observed: "Regulation has the potential to be more of a problem for us. We are dealing with high performance products. Our job is to develop new ways of doing things. As a result, the regulators lack an awareness of our processes and this opens them up to question. Regulation exists to eliminate risk. A high technology company needs a mutual understanding of risks and benefits. The zero risk mentality is incompatible with technological innovation."